The Dancing Dementia Dude

An Urgent Conversation
Between Dementia Folks,
Care Partners, and God

by
Dallas Dixon, the Dementia Dude

The Dancing Dementia Dude

Copyright © 2017 Dallas Dixon

Published by
North v west is stupid: gangs suck. ⚡

www.DancingDementiaDude.com

Editing by Ariel Dixon and Cheryl Brackett

Book design by Deborah Perdue,
Illumination Graphics

Softcover ISBN: #978-0-9986803-0-9

A Note from the Author

The book is comprised of real-life stories that describe early and middle stage dementia from my perspective—that of a man who has been diagnosed with Alzheimer's/Vascular dementia in 2014.

In my own experience, much of the first-person writing regarding dementia—while useful and often poignant—tends to focus on the grimmer side of the disease. It is my ambition then, to chronicle the humorous and opportunity-rich aspects of dementia, in hopes that it may inspire those affected to see a glimpse of light where there is often much gloom.

My journey thus far has not been without its darker days, but I have also been witness to delightful surprises and joyously humbling moments. The aim of these stories is to become a point of interaction between folks with dementia and their loved ones, to not only share personal experience but also to open a doorway into the little-known world of dementia—and perhaps have some fun along the way.

At a number of places in the book, I've included a page for reflection, conversation, and prayer. Some suggested questions are also included as a starting point. Questions to me are welcomed at gdmaine7@gmail.com.

Acknowledgments

There are many folks to thank, but I'll begin by honoring Christine Bryden, who wrote *Dancing with Dementia.* I only discovered her groundbreaking memoir after the initial titling of my own book, but after reading her work, I am moved to thank her for her wholehearted and discerning offering to the dementia community and its families. She was and continues to be a groundbreaker who opened the door for dementia folks to be involved in their own advocacy.

To my wife, Sonia, I thank God for your patience, perseverance, partnership and perspective. As much as I'd like to pretend, I'm not from Trenton, but the best girl in town married me. You are a wife and mother unequaled. To Boo, you are always the best in the fourth quarter, overachieving every mountain climb. I know the sensitive heart you are. To Bell, my editor and collaborator, you are a gentle spirit who wondered aloud at eight, the age of the oldest bible character. A prodigal daughter who never left home, while weaving the muses as if they came from a place few visit—thank you for your help throughout this endeavor.

To Kayla, your thirst for living echoes your father's and would make him proud. You have more than survived and you will continue to do so. To Sara, as you unravel your meaning in the world, it turns more heads in admiration than all the others. Remember your gentleness and empathy for others; with all of your successes to come, it will keep you humble.

A special and heartfelt thanks to my friends Cheryl Brackett, Irwin Stoolmacher, and Gwen Mitchell for their insight, edits, and endless support. To Pastor Bruce and his wife, mom, and the men in our men's group—thanks for listening. Thanks to Winston Young and Philip Barton for reaching out in truth and love. Lawyer Lisa and Richard Corey, your weekly visits were just plain fun and kept my spirit going. Lastly, thank you to Dr. Newman for being an insightful and caring physician who God used to give me another crack at life.

Table of Contents

Prologue

Knowing you are going to die forces you to take care of life's business. That sentence may come off a little silly. We're all going to die, right? But when your death is a bit scripted—when your malady has no cure—death comes into sharper focus. It's harder to put those end-of-life decisions on the back burner when the stove is turned on and the water is boiling, so to speak. A diagnosis of dementia allows the rare and coveted opportunity to handle these important decisions before it is too late, and to thus relieve some of the burdens on our loved ones, as well.

I also get the chance to clean up loose ends in relationships: forgive the sibling, appreciate the friend, get my marriage right, and tackle the bucket list of I wish I had. Many people do not get forewarning enough to address these things.

Here is the coolest thing. I am able to take time to appreciate going home to heaven before I actually go. I am able to contemplate the crossover and get into spiritual shape for the journey. I know that this concept is not universal, especially to those who do not believe in God. But at the very least, there is time enough to consider where you stand on spiritual matters. The sense of urgency that comes with a diagnosis of dementia helps oil the engine of that question we all carry: What is this life all about?

In other ways, too, dementia is an underrated disease. My world is smaller and thus my expectations are less; kindnesses and moments of joy are amplified. My ungodly and abrasive competitive streak that once ran rampant during my younger years has now, necessarily, mellowed. I know that I cannot win arguments anymore, so by default, I rarely compete. For me and mine, that is an extremely positive development. It goes without saying that there is much to this disease that is devastating to the body and mind, and especially to the loved ones that stand beside us throughout. I am sorry for them. But we dementia folks can still enjoy a good laugh, a good meal, music, a red sunset, a gentle touch, a kiss upon the forehead. They are made sweeter in their simplicity.

CHAPTER 1:

My Dearest Dementia

Dementia is a fat and narcissistic pig elbowing his way into five million U.S. families. Sadly, that number will triple by 2050. The pig thought he succeeded in taking over my life upon my diagnosis of Alzheimers'/vascular dementia in 2014. I almost thought so, too. I thought what went before was over and gone, and the future had been taken prisoner, put behind bars, accompanied by a divorce from family, work, and life as I knew it. What seemed to remain was nothing but a waiting game, populated by hopelessness, cognitive confusion, language disability, and memory loss. I was set to become the classic vegetable, without even a full knowledge of what that might mean.

I think that most of the common assumptions regarding dementia are one-sided, rooted in doom and gloom. It's blasphemy to say, but the truth is I have never been happier since I have had dementia. Oh, yes, I thought I was going to die within months. I intimated to my wife that she needed to learn to live on her own and start looking for a new husband. Without her knowledge, I put a deposit down on a nursing home with a memory care unit. Guess I got a little ahead of myself, huh? Dr. Neurologist wasn't much help; his only advice was…well, there wasn't any. His only question was—do you want to come back in six months, or twelve?

Of course, I have toxic days where my brain is extremely emotionally sensitive, and tears fall at the drop of a hat. And, I admit: irritability, paranoia, and a cold streak sometimes rear their ugly heads. To my love, I'm sorry. But for me, there are no deadlines from the law office or the charter school. The kids are out making their own way. Sonia does the bills (thank you) and the driving (thank you), except when Uber or Lyft is around. Time is mine again. These days I'm slower, but I can exercise, write, listen to music, and have long conversations with my wife and long texts with the girls. I can sleep when I need to. I can resolve old issues of pride, truthfulness, faith, friendship, and the addictions of work and drugs that weighed me down and made me ugly (thank you again, Sonia, for your divine patience). I can aim to reconcile with past relationships and wrong decisions through offering forgiveness or—more often than not—asking for it. God has become my best friend. I can reflect on doing God's work going forward, prayerfully and joyfully (says my tattoo). I can reflect on the law offices of Blackburn and Dixon, and the Emily Fisher Charter School, and renew those friendships. I can take time to see God trying to work in my life.

Dementia is full of opportunity. Its sinister nature is real, but it is not the whole story—just like my story doesn't begin or end with Alzheimer's/Dementia. My favorite dementia writer, Christine Bryden, wrote *Dancing with Dementia*. Her spirit leads me to continue to take the sting from dementia, and to redefine it as a disease of opportunity. It has begun to teach me lessons, and even give me joy. In her book she writes: "Each person with dementia is traveling a journey deep into the core of their spirit, away from the complex cognitive outer layer that once defined them through their life experiences, into the center of their being, in what truly gives them meaning in life." *Dancing with Dementia*, pg. 11.

"So much has been given to me;
I have no time to ponder
over that which has been denied."

Helen Keller

CHAPTER 2:

The First Time

The first time it happened was Saturday, March 14, 2015. It lasted momentarily, just about as long as it takes to pronounce the word. Then it was over. But, I won't forget it—an ironic statement to dementia folks.

The moment had a thickness to it. There was no color. Just before a little bit of panic sets in, the fluttering slow motion movie reel catches and starts up again. Reality floods back in as if nothing happened at all. But, it did. I didn't know who my wife Sonia was even though I saw her just a few steps ahead of me. Was this the beginning of things to come?

Sonia and I were finishing up errands after I had been to a funeral for Mrs. Moore, a mentor of mine.

Mrs. Moore had perfected one of those stern looks that make you sit up straight. Her patented combination of folded arms, tilted head, and steely eyes that penetrated any resolve had me confessing to things I didn't even do, just to make the room warm again. At the funeral home, I saw Mrs. Moore's buddy, Mrs. Smarr, some eighty years old. I got up to say hello and as I approached her, her daughter— who was tending to her—said, this is Dallas. I knew then that she was one of us.

In the supermarket parking lot, Sonia got out of the driver's side, me from the passenger's side. As we headed towards the store to pick up a few things, Sonia was—as usual—a few steps ahead of me. I looked up and saw a woman in her mid-fifties: black hair, about five-and-a-half feet tall, light skin with a beige tint you could only identify as Latin if you knew to look for it. I didn't recognize her. At all. I squinted my mind's eye and after a moment, she became Sonia again.

Is this what Mrs. Smarr sees much of the time? Physically, all the parts are there, fitting together quite ordinarily. But absent is the meaning these parts once possessed, when memory saw more than just a human being, but a person carrying fully the flavor of life—essences, memories attached, trust and feelings of closeness, intimacy, rich in nuance that warms with recognition.

It's like Mrs. Moore is giving that look of hers but to someone over my shoulder. And when I turn, no one is there. The physical action is clear, but it is devoid of meaning. I feel a twinge of panic, which returns on occasion. It better not be happening so quickly, Sonia says. Her worries have deep roots. My worries are minimal in comparison.

The experience is so otherworldly that I don't fault myself for thinking that maybe I just made it all up in my head. That I didn't see what I saw. That I don't really have dementia. Or maybe my head made the moment up in order to help me. To get me ready; to get Sonia and I ready. If so, my head is treating me kindly. And maybe, it's God, showing me kindness and gentleness to prepare me for a world that operates like this all the time.

– Discussion, Thoughts, and Prayers –

1. What was the diagnosis experience like for you?

2. How did you tell your loved ones, and how did they respond?

CHAPTER 3:

Dream Life

With dementia, self-diagnosis is inherently suspect. All self-observations are tinted by forgetfulness, or suffer from disorganization, or are simplistic and fragmented analyses laced with an emotionality that often has a life of its own.

My case of dementia is moving at a quick pace, and as a result, my window of cogency falls typically within the hours before 10 a.m. If I'm up early enough, that window can be substantial. But after that, I'm mentally full—unable and therefore unwilling (not the other way around) to process, analyze, and strategize. When I sleep, it's for rather long periods of time—nine hours a night, three hours during the day. But it's starting to be something I look forward to because my dreams are rich, specific, and full of satisfying emotion and accomplishment.

Last night, for instance, I dreamt I was back at the Fisher Charter school. I was organizing an assembly with all its component parts—moving the kids around using the right amount of joy, armed with the right amount of staff, provided even with the right amount of satisfaction, when the jigsaw puzzle came together. It's a simple dream-world accomplishment, that comes with no sense of dread, or embarrassment, or futility in its enjoyment.

It's been four years since Emily Fisher Charter School closed. The memories of those fifteen years are pretty much mush in my head as my dementia progresses. And four years is a long time. But, dementia is subtle—eating away at the number and clarity of the memories. Unless I am dreaming.

It's almost as if time gone by has set up camp in my brain, way down deep where dreams wait for me to sleep. The dreams about the school not only have me cognitively alert and multitasking, but they are so kind in the storyline. The school is never closed down. It's fully operational and without dread. The dream reconciles fact and fiction by creating a scenario that the New Jersey Department of Education has given us another chance, both willingly and because they have lost their paperwork, and the new managers aren't aware that we are staying beyond our welcome. Sure, in my Fisher dreams I may be feeling overwhelmed a bit from the responsibility of it all, but I'm alive. I'm in the game and enjoying the fight.

So as my dementia progresses, my dreams have become kinder and gentler, and less stressful. Gone are the once ruthless stress dreams that demanded even more angst than the real life they mimicked. There are no more repeat viewings of dreams that had me mid-escape from a prison camp. No more taking off into the back woods, covering my tracks as I went, attempting to out-strategize the authorities. No changing clothes, diverting towards an unexpected direction, hitching around the bend with the police close at hand.

Instead, dementia has ironically settled whatever emotional motivator once drove those escape dreams, either through loss of memory or perhaps loss of stress.

Another one of my old standby stress dreams went like this. It's me, outside the registrar's office at Princeton University. I have been enrolled there for years—nine, even ten years perhaps. During this unusually lengthy stretch, I have somehow already been to law school though I haven't yet finished my undergraduate degree at Princeton—a dream enabled impossibility, of course. I'm considering going out for the soccer team after all these years, but I know I need to get in shape. Other students are amazed I'm still here, but the registrar hasn't given up on me.

For years these dreams have me going into the registrar's office hoping they won't give me the boot for taking so long to graduate. Always, the paperwork in my file is voluminous, so much so that the registrar can't resolve it on the spot. Go to class, they suggest. Stop skipping, they say, and I do. But recently I had another repeat of this dream. After years of tossing and turning as I watched the same stressful plot points tick by, the narrative I'd spent a lifetime dreaming finally changed. I make it to the registrar's office, and this time there is no overflowing stack of papers, no exasperated registrar insisting I stop skipping class. In this most recent dream, the university has lastly decided to digitize their records. The registrar tells me in relief that I've finally graduated. Dementia has changed the ending. This time, all is well.

*"Happiness is to appreciate what you have;
unhappiness is to dwell on
what you don't have."*

Rabbi Shimon Ben Zoma (2nd century)

— Discussion, Thoughts, and Prayers —

1. What are your dreams like these days?

2. How can you worship God if you can't remember who God is for you?

CHAPTER 4:

Virtual Dementia Tour

Really? Is there such a thing? There is, and I went on it. Though I have to admit, I probably wasn't their favorite passenger. Here's the story.

I showed up at the nursing home that was running these virtual dementia tours by appointment. I'm sure they thought they were cutting edge—and who knows, maybe they are, but not because of that virtual dementia tour. To be fair, I'm pretty sure that the dementia tour wasn't really designed for someone like me—that is to say, someone with dementia. But, at the time I thought, maybe I'll get a jump on things, and went to check it out.

I was in the first group of three ready to begin the tour at 9:30 a.m. The two ladies in my group were not dementia folks, for sure. Perhaps they were caregivers or professionals in the field? Whatever their reasons for attending, they were easily compliant with the instructions. I was not.

"Put on these gloves. It will simulate arthritis, which makes it hard to grasp things," the social worker at the nursing home said with a smile. "My bosses say I am good with folks with dementia," she told us in her introduction. "I just make them believe I am their friend and then I can get them to do most anything." I'm paraphrasing here a bit, but not by much.

I said, "No gloves for me. I just want to do the dementia stuff."

A weird look.

"Okay, well, put these rubber-spiked insoles inside your shoes to simulate neuropathy of the feet."

The ladies took off their shoes and inserted the insoles.

"No thanks," I said.

Then came the glasses meant to represent macular degeneration.

"Nope."

Then there were the earphones that blasted muffled sounds, while the social worker gave directions.

"I can't hear," I told her. She told me later that I wasn't supposed to.

A little trick, she joked. "I didn't want you to think I was being mean," she explained.

Anyway, into the dark room I went, decked out in the earphones, ready to undertake the instructed five assigned tasks in five minutes, which would be exceptionally difficult to accomplish since I couldn't hear her tell me the tasks in the first place. Did I mention there was a strobe light?

I surrendered. I didn't want to play anymore. I parked myself in a chair. I couldn't have done one task, and at that point, I had no desire to try. It was too hard. So, I sat until I figured out that I didn't have to be miserable and subject myself to this. I took off the headphones and left.

Maybe it taught me more than I thought.

Driving home, I wondered—is advanced dementia that debilitating? A truth which was buried was exposed, which is a worthwhile thing, but I also wondered why there was such a big effort by the Alzheimer's Community to make things seem dead and dismal. Was their virtual dementia tour a tease of emotional manipulation in order to spur some fundraising? The wonder remains.

CHAPTER 5:

Walking (or Spinning) with Purpose

B ased on that title, I bet you think this chapter is going to be all heavy and philosophical, or even—heaven forbid—spiritual. I would have thought the same thing. Oh great, another sermon from someone who sees himself as more righteous than broken. And when I say broken, I'm talking about one's awareness of how far he or she has fallen short in pleasing God and in treating others the right way.

That digression aside, in this chapter I am talking about literally walking with purpose. Man, does it make me feel great. We with dementia sometimes come across things that make us feel more connected to an older, familiar version of aliveness—like we've found the secret cure that somehow all the doctors missed or forgot (irony intended) to tell us about. Somehow to work physically towards something, to be connected physiologically with a purpose provides a mental clarity and relief.

I asked three neighbors if I could cut their lawns, for nothing. I could see their assessments washing over their faces. 'Will he ask for money later?' 'Will he quit after five minutes? Will he mess things up? Will he become a leach—too close, too involved? Do I really want to sign up for this kind of unknown?' I must have passed their test, because I am now responsible for four lawns, including my own patch. When I venture by their lawns, I do my own assessment—and boy, do they look good. Then again, sometimes it's oops, missed a spot.

I've also learned about oil and gas, weed whackers, trimming, dips in the ground, and rock dangers. Is this great, or what? For the rest of the day, I feel almost normal, not flu-like in my head, not disoriented. And to top that, Sonia got me spinning classes—that's riding a stationary bike indoors at different speeds and inclines. Exercise is my own special medication. If I ride an hour, twice a day, I feel almost normal. Feelings of thick-headedness reduce, and my memory seems to function, albeit at a slower pace. Every single nursing home and every single adult day care center should have exercise opportunities.

Then, there's music. It touches down via a separate portal to our demented brains. Music provides free joy without overload or fatigue. I recently went to a ukulele group, and the first song we learned was "Hang Down Your Head Tom Dooley," which I had once memorized off of my brother's 45 record player. To this day it is the first and only song that I remember almost all the lyrics to, and it's also the same song I taught my kids during car rides. You should have seen me strumming along. I was completely happy—and completely not following the beat or correct chords. I ended up giving my ukulele back because it was too hard for my new brain (and probably my old brain as well).

That's the final piece to the phrase the Alzheimer's folk's use: "living well with dementia." The joy that stemmed from the ukulele club's chosen song, an apparent coincidence, was actually God giving me an unexpected ice cream cone. Kindness in the unexpected is surely a gift from God.

1. Do other health issues get in the way of living well with Dementia? What about other medications? Alcohol? Marijuana?

2. What are your ten favorite songs, pictures, verses that you can enjoy regularly?

CHAPTER 6:

Dementia and Marriage

I have avoided writing this one. I've avoided it like the plague. A recurring theme in my recent writing is this: that dementia is really not so bad, and it even has attractive—almost tantalizing—upsides. That is until you get to what the disease does, or could do to a marriage.

Caveat: a standard saying in dementia circles is that everyone—every family, every caregiver, every marriage—experiences the disease differently. So, I must hereby invoke that message and disclaim that these marriage observations are my own, and are not meant to be an instruction manual or end-all-be-all chronicle. You got that, right?

When you have dementia, you change like crazy. Let's start there. Cognitively, you become very different. Your memory starts to go, beginning in the most recent sphere and then moving backward. Your thinking skills change. I laugh to myself when I say I will never win another argument with my wife. I just can't think fast enough to keep up. I can't synthesize the points that she is making, analyze them from my perspective, and then design a response that matches her inquiry or challenge in enough time. To analogize this predicament: the argument has left the airport without me on the plane; Sonia is playing in the third quarter and I'm just finishing up the first. Not to mention that I am developing what they call aphasia – the inability to speak fluently. It also means I am developing an inability to fully process words that are coming at me.

Here's an additional secret that dementia people think they keep well hidden but in actuality their wives and husbands know all too well: we tend to hit the emotional accelerator about certain issues, while the car is still in park.

I think this behavior is indicative of an unconscious knowledge that we no longer control a lot of our goings-on, and when we hook on an issue, an argument, a worry, we think it might be the last fish, or better yet—we haven't caught a fish in quite a while, so we are going to be overly careful to land this one.

All that is to say, that the here-and-now, important emotional interactions are all tangled up in dementia. The dementia person can't keep up and doesn't want to admit it, and his or her spouse, of course, can't read minds. Your spouse can't tell if you are fully tracking, not tracking at all, being a usual amount of stubborn, obtuse, prideful, emotional, or the elevated dementia levels of stubborn, obtuse, prideful and emotional. It's sort of like the dementia spouse is speaking two languages that both sound like English, but the normal spouse can't discern when each is being spoken. Makes you not want to have an argument, huh? Of course not. But, then it begins—the slow, emotionally-strangling process of disengagement from the present.

As simple an interaction as 'Do you want any coffee, honey?' begins to beg investigatory and sometimes tangentially related questions. I'm trying to strategically manage these lines of thinking—is the coffee hot...What are we about to do?...Will the coffee hide what I was getting ready to do?...Is she having another cup?......Is there enough left? A non-dementia person may have these thoughts, too, but

you can synthesize them quickly, coming to con-
clusions or throwing away the unimportant and
irrelevant. Not so, in my case.

The normal here-and-now is compromised and
will become more so. There is a holding on to the
normal here-and-now that couples fall into, the
comfortable routines of various importance. For
us, we play cards. Gin rummy. My ability to work
with numbers and sense, or to calculate probabil-
ities in getting a matching card has always been
first rate. Not so anymore. But the game gives her
peace. My joy in calculating the odds and then it
turning out the way I expected is still fun, but in
memory only.

Sleeping is different. I take multiple naps sometimes
and as such, the night sleeping can be fitful, and I
end up waking her up. She's not the world's sound-
est sleeper, so that can become a problem. Then
there's the social world: friends, multiple conversations, discussing current events, family functions,
weddings, watching TV together, going to the
movies. All here-and-now stuff that has curdled for
me, leaving her married to a different guy. The stock
response is, well, you've always been different.
Correct, but now I'm a different-different. The
now-Dallas who was different from the world is

now different from himself, different from his own definition as husband as defined by the first thirty-two years of our marriage. I'm enjoying the change, but why would any spouse?

The spouse thinks, he is changing fast. It's the disease, dementia, I hate it. I want the old Dallas back. The one I've grown old with. I can't have him back so I'll do the best I can helping him manage the disease. The downside is that approach makes me a dependent – you the parent, me the child. The trick is staying in the here-and-now, enjoying the slower and simpler things that still register with the new Dallas, like music, a good view, a good laugh, exercise, slow mulling conversation (that is slow but not stupid).

Past memory is damaged late in dementia, so that reflections on, and pictures of the past can be exhilarating. Not only does it bring back normal memories, it is actually encouraging to the demented person to share equally. Past stuff can be teary. That's okay, too. Emotional moments can be exhausting, but cleansing.

The future is the dragon. I don't know the answers, but I believe that the dementia spouse can and should participate in long-term planning. Visit the nursing homes that may be available. Discuss the standards of care that he wants and how to monitor a system that cannot be trusted to always do the right thing. Medical powers of attorney, fiscal power of attorney, and wills, are critical cornerstones to planning that should be done jointly. Planning the funeral, together—maudlin as it may sound—is a good thing, in my book.

Now I remember the all-important vow: "till death do us part, in sickness and in health." I believed it when I made that vow, and I believe it now. When I was first diagnosed, I thought about a divorce—not for me, but for her. To free her from the tentacles of a cognitively disabled husband. But who am I to mess with her vows before God anyway? And maybe that's not what she wants. Duh. What an overreaction, demented dude.

The goal? Stay married, of course. Embrace the change with the same humble knowledge that we will make many mistakes and hurt the feelings of our spouse, demented or not. We must forgive them and ask for forgiveness, rely on them, and be thankful for all that remains—beauty, gentleness, humor, music, joy, a sunset, blueberry muffins, slow musings on the past, cathartic moments in the present, where fixing it all is not the goal, but sharing all is. Praying together is also helpful, because it puts our needs, our worries, our thankfulness, and any spiritual war-fare in God's hands, not our own. Probably that's where it should have been all along. He doesn't take a vacation from His children, as hardheaded as we are. He is patient and loving, offering mercy, grace, and answered prayers at every turn.

The future—when heaven is figured into the deal—stymies the angst and worry, some. It reminds us that we are just visiting here, that our home is to come, one without tears, where we will be with our spouse forever.

'How're you doing?' I'm asked.

I say, 'The best is yet to come.'

— Discussion, Thoughts, and Prayers —

1. What marriage routines will you maintain and which will you discard? What new ones will you create together?

CHAPTER 7:

Dementia and Sanctification

This may be pure supposition, but here it goes. Sanctification is when God cleans you up, step-by-step, after you have accepted His invitation to be a child of God. If you are not that interested in this concept, feel free to skip the more formal definitions below:

Sanctifying: to make holy, set apart as sacred, to purify or free from sin. Progressively becoming like Jesus...sanctification is used as a post-reformation theological term to refer to the ongoing process of Christian growth...the original Greek word is often translated into English as "wash" or "cleanse."

Everybody agrees: dementia is different for everyone. But here's what I think about mine. First, it was a little ironic that I spent my whole professional life flaunting my cognitive abilities—analysis, multitasking, endless hours, millions of quick decisions under pressure, defending myself against the world, full of pride—only to have this disease undermine my excessive pride in my thinking ability. Although it will cause much consternation in the transition from the old Dallas to the new, that is not a tragedy. From a spiritual perspective, it's one less sin to carry—a victory!

When I was a lawyer and a teacher, my arts were speaking, advocacy, fast thinking, and manipulation. And so another irony rears its head. The second major dementia symptom I've experienced has been the decline in my ability to speak. The bottom line is this: there are no more arguments to win. Neither is that a tragedy. Instead, gentleness seeps in. Competition is no longer possible. Considering whether what I have to say is pleasing to God is much easier at this slower place. A gift, not a tragedy.

And, of course, I'm an Eagles fan. I bleed green. I can no longer watch TV with the sound on. My TV addiction and sports addiction—relying on them for peace instead of God—is the next sin removed.

Dementia is liberating. Who would have thought?

Jesus looked at them and said,
"With man this is impossible, but with God
all things are possible."

Matthew 19:26

CHAPTER 8:

Moments of Protection

Real danger was afoot and I never knew it. The kind of situations that leave you publically humiliated, in jail, or dead. I didn't know who God was, other than what the word was meant to connote—you know, the guy with the long white beard who sits above the clouds, mostly disappointed, shaking his head or his fist in anger. Heaven: a great place to go to after you die. If you try hard, and your batting percentage is worthy, you are in. I thought I was special, that I could handle the world, but I hardly knew what was happening or how close to danger I was flying, as if immune.

So, my safety was hardly due to smarts or cunning. Even if you turn your nose up at my type of God,

I simply can't. It would be so much easier to believe in hitting the lottery multiple times. The odds are too farfetched. I know God is farfetched too, I get it. The Virgin Mary, people dying and coming back to life, a God caring for each of his 7 billion. And there's more—God talking to us, us talking to God. C'mon, man. And what kind of God is he? With all the bad stuff going on? And I know this Pastor, Priest, Rabbi, Reverend or Imam who's a phony! And God, why does he have to be the Father? Why not Mother? Religion is so screwed up. Why would I—why would any-one—put all their eggs in that basket?

I had no choice. What was going on outside and inside—there was no other explanation. And then it kept making more and more sense—to love your enemies; to give gifts to people who didn't deserve it, grace. God acted opposite of everything I was taught, but His way is starting to make sense. Here is my Letterman Top Ten God Saved My Butt Moments that Humbled Me to My Knees.

10. Late one evening, I was meeting with clients at my law offices in Trenton. Everyone else had gone home. My office was on the second floor and I had come down to see if anyone was still waiting to be seen. There was a man

I had never seen before. After some exchange, he left and went down the street. He proceeded to rob and rough up a lawyer at the next office, according to the newspaper the next morning.

9. At the height of my illusions, I told my seven-year-old nephew to hold on to my neck and we would swim across the lake. 100 yards out, it came to me suddenly that I had nothing left. No strength, no options. I was trying to hold him up over my head. I couldn't call out. Help came out off the point in the last second.

8. I was an ambulance-chaser for many of my early law years. I hired a guy, Barnabus, who was a leader in the Haitian community to direct clients to me. I suspected many accidents were cooked up. I never spoke about it, but I suspected—more than suspected—and played dumb. The prosecutor who was looking to indict me on insurance fraud met with Barny. Nothing went farther.

7. She was my girlfriend in college. We did drugs. She passed out cold. I panicked, she woke up.

6. When I ran for office, the prosecutor asked my campaign worker whether people were using drugs in the campaign headquarters. They were. I was. They never came.

5. In high school, I thought it was hilarious to bomb down a windy hill at a crazy speed with my buddies howling in real fear until I missed an oncoming car. I don't know how I didn't die or kill someone.

4. A truck was barreling down Perry Street through the light. Or was I in the wrong? It was impossible to get out of the way. No accident. It was a miracle. Believe that.

3. Driving to West Virginia late at night, I'm in the passenger seat, out cold. Sonia, the love of my life, is driving. I wake up exactly as the car started to swerve off the road. I grabbed the wheel in milliseconds. I don't remember if the kids were with us. The hugeness of the miracle made it impossible to process, but the timing couldn't have happened otherwise. When it's like that, it's God. I know it now.

2. In college, I visited my high school buddy, Rick, who would die early of alcoholism. We took LSD and ended up at a creek to go

swimming after an impossible car ride. I dove off a bridge from six feet up and should have died because there was only three feet of water. Instead, I tore up my head with multiple stitches. But, I should have died.

1. In the law office days, I got a call one afternoon from Prosecutor Cindy. I went over to her office to see what was up. There was a tall African-American dude sitting at one end of the desk that she was behind. I scouted him. They were about to beat down the doors of my offices with cops and newspapers in tow because the dude had made an undercover buy of heroin packaged in my office's letterhead envelopes. I lost all color. It could have been scandalous front page news for weeks. I could have lost way more, never to recover.

All are a matter of what could have been, but God protects even though I never gave him the time of day. If the Creator was faithful, then how much more now in the dementia world.

*"joyful prayerful thankful
waiting on u my God."*

Dallas the Dementia Dude's tattoo

CHAPTER 9:

My First Miracle

The surveys, you probably know, say that most people believe in miracles. A miracle doesn't mean that an event is strictly supernatural, and it certainly doesn't mean said event was instigated by the Creator of the Universe or the God spoken of in any of the Holy Books. Some people might just use the word to mean extraordinary luck or one-in-a-million odds.

I was recently remembering my first big miracle and my eye began to tear. It was a dazzling memory, seared indelibly in my mind—a memory so solid perhaps, that it would be cool if it survived the progression of dementia.

The time: spring of 1970, close to midnight. The place: Princeton University, outside Alexander Hall. The event: the Board of Trustees and the University Governing Body were meeting to debate and decide whether to close the university and suspend exams in reaction to President Nixon escalating the war in Vietnam and crossing into Cambodia. Me: a freshman participating in the erupting Anti-War movement. My Dad: a Trustee on the University Board.

My father didn't speak during the deliberations, and I didn't tell my fellow protestors of my connection to a voting member because I wasn't sure what his position was or how he was going to vote. The building was packed, Roman coliseum style—a round balcony over-flowing with students, voicing pleasure and displeasure with the decision-makers seated below. The board did not perceptibly acknowledge the hundreds of unofficial jurors, but of course, they knew we were there. The hall was electric.

The time came to vote. Strike or no strike; yes or no. Others were counting the votes as they were cast openly and verbally, called by name, one at a time. Down the line arrived my father's turn to cast his vote.

"Mr. Dixon, how do you vote?"

"Yes."

Yes? Did my Dad just vote to strike? He did. Okay, Pop! Now it was easy to tell the others of my connection. It was a vote that mattered most to me. Ultimately, the Board voted to strike by a little less than a comfortable margin. The crowd was ecstatic!

I headed out of the steamy meeting hall, about to head right but veered left to avoid the swelling crowd. I almost bumped right into his chest. My father and I were toe-to-toe amidst the mass. He was so happy. I was so proud of him. We looked at each other with joy and wonder, and exchanged a few meaningless words—what else can you do when a miracle unfolds? You are small, the miracle is big.

— Discussion, Thoughts, and Prayers —

1. What miracles could you all pray for?

2. Do you keep track of God's answers?
   It's pretty cool.

CHAPTER 10:

What Drives Caregivers

A year before I was diagnosed, Sydney Fisher—my dad's half-brother—died after nine years in a medical care facility. He had dementia resulting from a stroke. He was also a musician of some renown—singing, arranging, and piano-playing at the Orpheus Club in Philadelphia. He didn't have any children. Instead, his will called for his estate to be managed by my sister, who died from uterine cancer, before Syd's stroke. So, I was the backup guy. Without knowing about dementia or strokes, and really not knowing how to be a caregiver, I became his caregiver for nine years.

It was not until I was diagnosed with my own dementia that I remembered I had once been on the other side of things; the caregiver, rather than the one cared for. I wanted to remember both the good and bad, so that I might pass some knowledge on to other caregivers and to folks living with any form of the fifty various conditions that cause dementia.

Sydney had a Ph.D. in electrical engineering. He was a computer whiz before Silicon Valley was really on the map, but when I offered, as his caregiver, to put simple programs on his computer for his use, he'd say to me, "Too much, too much."

But, let's take the caregiver's mask off. Caregiving is not simply about the everyday battles—managing the meds, keeping the bathroom clean. There are internal battles, too, within caregivers themselves. The lives of caregivers have been completely upended. Imagine you become the caregiver to your husband. Instead of living out the dream of growing old together, you suddenly have two full-time jobs: the regular day job or career required for financial support and the money involved in taking care of your spouse; the additional full-time job of caregiving, which has no salary, no punch clock, no paid leave. If it was politically correct, we would likely scream at the top of our lungs, "Why me, God? My life was just beginning again! The kids are finally grown! We were supposed to have a little freedom! Now I have to take care of this guy for five years, or maybe twenty, and he's not even the same guy I married."

My lowest moment, the instance when I was least proud of myself, occurred while taking care of Sydney. Somehow I managed to be self-centered while standing next to a guy who, though he could barely speak, managed to say thank you to everyone. He was in a wheelchair, living in a hospital, seeing few others, all of whom he may not have remembered the second they left the room. To myself, I'd say, I'm tired, I want to go home, maybe he'll be asleep early. Syd, I would rationalize, is closer to the aids and nurses than he is to me. I'm just another manager. What am I going to do here, he can't speak, I'm not sure he is or wants to track me.

Meanwhile, Syd played the piano daily for the other residents during their singing time, until even he could hear a missed note. Heartbreaking for a pianist, right? I struggled to deal with the doctors, handle Syd's tangential health issues. Firstly, wrangling these matters was time-consuming—stroke recovery, body massages, physical therapy to continue to walk and exercise, cutting his toenails, changing his diaper, wiping his butt, skin cancer, minor related surgeries, high blood pressure, and diabetes. It was difficult dealing with the professional caregivers, eight of whom I fired for faking their duties or not telling the truth. To add to that, you often had to be stealthy in discerning the effectiveness of the aids, since they'd often cover for each other.

And then a funny thing happened. Syd became my best friend. We learned to communicate by gestures and tone of voice. I could translate the grunts. There was a magnificent world inside Syd that was no longer cognitively based. Gentleness, perseverance, gratitude, and patience were what you held hands with. Watching the joy on his face at the Orpheus concerts or riding around in the car in Maine was contagious. Of course, I made big mistakes along the way, but a turning point came when I learned to be in the moment with Syd, and to not discount small joys and minor victories.

I hope that my wife and children will be able to admit to and laugh about the inconvenience, grossness, the time consumption, and the emotionally taxing nature of caregiving. I hope they are able to remember all the godly moments along the way, so they don't lose their redemptive power.

Sonia tells me the look in my eyes is changing, that I don't care about my appearance. I can't play

Scrabble anymore or watch T.V. I get overly fixated and emotional about small stuff—that we don't have laundry detergent. My social filters are crumbling, which can be funny but can also be embarrassing and shameful. I sleep during the day, but not at night. I cling to routine like a baseball caught in the left field seats. But I can still tell a good story—if I write notes, first. I am generally kind. I love my wife. I love God, and love to talk about how he moves in our lives. I can give good back rubs. We share our kids, Maine, and thirty-three years of memories, good and bad.

Syd showed me how to be thankful and joyful in dementia.

CHAPTER 11:

Bobo the Demented Clown

The face paint was a draw for me. I read somewhere that every clown had his or her own distinct makeup, depending in part on the type of clown character they chose to be. You know, the sad clown, the puzzled clown, the gregarious over-the-top clown. And then there was the clown nose that squeaked. Heavenly.

I started doing birthday parties at $35 a gig after I graduated college in 1975 or so. Shortly thereafter I added magic tricks to the mix, too. My act was a little bit of a hit—doing my own kids' parties, as well as those of family and friends, and even some church entertainment. Bobo the Clown Does Jesus Lessons—it couldn't be beat. My favorite trick was endlessly pulling a paper mache stream out of the ear of a seven-year-old, while commenting on his or her questionable ear-cleaning skills. I have even done one nightclub show, where I was so nervous I threw up in the bathroom before coming out. My disappearing act—using a toy quacking duck as my prop—was a complete and utter failure, resulting in me stepping on the poor thing (not silently).

At the start of each school year at Emily Fisher Charter School, I used to meet the kids with a welcome sign in full clown regalia. Purple feather plumes, white face paint with an exaggerated red smile going cheek to cheek, a red and white striped shirt and yellow pants, and big, black duck shoes. Some of the younger students would avoid my hello.

Clowns can be scary, thanks to the horror movie industry. But I would often manage a smile from them, using the disappearing duck, and then a bigger smile when I'd inevitably drop it or otherwise telegraph my trick in bumbling clown fashion. Reality and theater sort of began to merge, which was the greatest theater of all. Remaining cheerful or feigning upset at the failure of my disappearing act would be celebrated collaboratively between me and the student. The older the child, the more the connection—until ages 16 or 17, when appearances dominated all.

My clown stuff is all put away now—makeup, clown horn, flash paper (a favorite), all together in a big, lovely, musty clump in a duffle bag somewhere in the basement or attic. But, I wonder if I've put it away just a little too soon. My disappearing skills have made an unexpected comeback. At first, my wallet disappeared into a black hole under my napkin as I tried to pay for lunch at a restaurant. Suddenly, it was gone. And it mystified the crowd— really just me and the owner, who let me leave to search for it who knows where. Somehow my old magic skills had blossomed beyond all expectations. Then, another trick. My medical insurance card disappeared between the pages of a book, only to be found three days later when I resumed reading. No one could have figured out that one. There were other tricks of course: the frying pan in the bowl drawer was a good one. And I've also perfected the disappearing car key fob trick. I drove the car out of the garage and to the gym and with an abracadabra, the key was gone.

When I was Bobo the Clown, my final, death-defying trick was always the water in the pitcher. The trick pitcher I employed had a discreet insert to make it seem that it was full of milk. With a little nudging, the milk retreated to the bottom of the pitcher while I poured confetti on the person in the room who least wanted to volunteer. Now, as demented Bobo the Clown, my show-stopper is finding my glasses after they had gone up in smoke the day before. They were uncovered in the drawer that holds the coffee filters—an inexplicable sleight of hand, never before witnessed.

It makes me wonder if there should be dementia birthday parties, where dementia magicians could share their own reality-defying, mind-bending stories. Remembering my Bobo days has also got me thinking about reality and theater, and the magical moments in which they sometimes meet. I ran an idea by my wife recently: to hand out red clown noses at my funeral. She didn't go for it, as you might imagine, but I've still got a few tricks up my sleeve.

"May the God of hope
fill you with all joy and peace
as you trust in Him."

Romans 15:13

– Discussion, Thoughts, and Prayers –

1. What are the ten most joyful activities you now participate in? Small or big ones count.

2. Which ones are built into your routine?

CHAPTER 12:

"You Know I Love You?"

Such a beautiful thing to say to someone. When Sonia says it to Dallas, it travels into him, creating warmth and security. Without those words said periodically, over the course of our thirty-two-year marriage, there would only exist a cool cement room, full of life's goings-on but ultimately uninviting. The words are especially kind now. Dallas has dementia, and each utterance is meant to be a gentle reassurance.

In reality, the words ricochet. I try to catch up with them as they recede, then disappear. Dementia pulls away the threads of personality. I am different. My response can no longer be automatic – I love you, too. I am lost in the interpretation, aiming to reduce my response to its essence. There are always competing interests – we're busy: the job, the family, the dinner, the kids, the TV. But, when you have dementia the business of life slows down, enticing one to serious reflection, interpretation down to the slimmest degree of minutia.

Did she say:

"You know, I love you." Or…

"You, know I love you." Or…

"You know I love you?" Or…

"You know I love you!"

The potential for alternate meanings within each iteration causes disquiet. I cannot catch the bouncing ball. I am lost anticipating its next bounce; I don't know why I'm chasing it in the first place. I have no earthly idea why I haven't responded in an equally loving, kind, and assuring way—connecting with her. By the time I arrive at such a point, the conversation is long over and my silence evokes a little disquiet on her end, too. There is a gap between my desire and ability to fulfill it, which leads to a devastating, palms-up shrug that means I can no longer connect in the manner we'd grown to know.

Hours later, still stuck on it all, I wonder if I can love her in the same way I used to. I have to tread carefully here, because within the question exists a double-edged sword. Maybe I can't love her in the same way, but perhaps what I can no longer do is also the thing that damaged our love—being self-serving, prideful, not quiet, insincere. Maybe dementia, with all its limiting of ability, will limit my bad habits, too.

So, if I were to take my time unraveling—what would I say to her later on when I had the chance to cherish her words and construct my own? My first thought is: we have so much time, let's enjoy it. But this feels hollow. So I venture onward and arrive at: When you tell me "you know I love you," it means so much. It warms my heart and I know you are reassuring me about the difficult dementia times to come. I never doubt your perseverance. It was one of the reasons I fell in love with you and continue to love you today. When you get home, tonight, let's talk about it even more.

The words open up the floodgates—uncontrollable tears. Dementia sometimes has the power to make the tears easier to let loose, but if I'm being honest, I never knew how to close the floodgates once they opened. Sonia calls them the Dallas Weepies. Like then on the phone. Like now. I hang up. I stop here.

"Darkness deserves gratitude. It is the alleluia point at which we learn to understand that all growth does not take place in the sunlight."

Joan Chittister

CHAPTER 13:

The Uglies are Nasty

Praise God in the middle of the war? I tried, but my prayer seemed like a whisper, easily swept aside by the roaring of battle. On January 7, 2015, I asked my friends on Facebook for prayer, offering to return the favor with prayers of my own. I provided no details, it was simply a plea. It had become undeniably clear that I was losing the fight when relying solely on my own prayers. After making my social media plea, I put the phone down and fell asleep without any expectations. The confusion, directionless anger, agitated dismay—it felt as if I was waiting for defeat to become official.

I write this without the desire to evoke worry, or fear, or sympathy. My emotional, dementia-induced darkness was like an accelerator stuck, speeding by buildings and curves in the road, challenging my control. The darkness of dementia includes violence for some, directed at the loved ones who have sacrificed the most by dedicating themselves to caregiving. Thankfully, my dementia has never turned physical, but it could have, if not for prayer and perhaps medication. My war was ostensibly about how much power my wife needed to run my affairs, few as they may be. I urged her to make the managing less her priority, and instead allow me to manage my side of things on my own. It was about my perception that our marriage and I came second to her new life born of loneliness because I was living on my own in Maine for seven months.

This wasn't an intellectual war; it was one fought in the mud, fueled by the endlessly repetitious mental images of jealousy and distrust that seemed to prove the paranoia and led me lower—searching through cell phones and emails and desk drawers for smoking gun evidence.

In "She Belongs to Me," Bob Dylan sings of that perilous fall into disgrace and distrust. He sings that he is down on his knees, looking through the keyhole of her bedroom door. I knew my behavior was desperate, but I still attempted to mask it with a cold demeanor, that at once veered towards suspicion, then to flatness, then to sharpness. My dark days blew out from my soul like a nor'easter—and it surprised even me. And what was worse—I enjoyed the power and the corroded energy of it all, like a maniacal cartoon character, rubbing his hands together, with his head thrown back in an evil cackle.

Until this moment I thought I could handle bad times by myself. Be my own manager. Help from others was a sign of weakness. And help from God? Sure, that would be great, but I'm not expecting it really. God has better things to do, I thought. And I haven't done much for God lately. So where did I arrive? Some momentary prayer thrown powerlessly to heaven, like playing a lottery ticket—the glimmer of a promise, but little expectation of a win.

The year before my formal diagnosis, vague signs crossed my horizon unexplained. I was drafting a court affidavit in the last days of Fisher Prep and brought it to court, attempting to submit it, before I was informed that I had already drafted and submitted it. Then, in the early months following my diagnosis, I had trouble understanding why dementia folks and their loved ones told such dark, titanic stories. Though I still believe that dementia is full of hidden pleasures—and is certainly better than many physically painful diseases—year two, post-diagnosis, has caught me flatfooted. So came the Uglies, as I call them. I gave them that name because they are an emotional elixir of agitation, impatience, and distrust that rises to paranoia. To boot, it causes me to become overly sensitive, overly analytical, and overly conspiratorial—all while simultaneously overly confident of my own acuity, my own right-eousness, my own investigative prowess. (A dementia digression. LOL)

I searched phones. I checked messages. I concocted disingenuous conversations to illicit information. My mind raced. I slept rarely. I prayed for God to reveal the truth. I fasted for three days, the first with no water, the second two with no food. My anxiety grew exponentially, and there was no other reality. It was all of my day and night. I cycled endlessly without any new information, creating my own mental whirlpool of reality where even the innocuous transfigured into a smoking gun.

There were three separate episodes. The first issue of paranoia subsided when they looked me in the eye and told me they'd done nothing wrong. The second episode was smothered by four-hour bike rides, praying on and off most of the way. The third episode was the perfect storm. That's when God gave me the wisdom to turn away from my own prayers, and reach out to the others, even online. And so I slept. When I awoke, the Uglies had lifted, thanks to the prayers of hundreds of friends who had received my call, had returned it with prayer. I came to with a relief not unlike escaping a bad psychedelic trip back in the sixties. I felt empty and tired, but free from the mental domination of the Uglies.

The subject of my paranoia, my mental target, told me I had scared them. All the other folks involved in the dysfunctional intrigue had gone away. Their demeanor was no longer dubious or I no longer misread it. The relationship had reverted without an aftertaste or remnant of any kind. It's been ten days since the Uglies and I feel as if the world has adjusted itself back on its axis.

Suffice it to say that this is not one of those dementia opportunities that is something to be upbeat about. Here are the facts. One-third of dementia folks become aggressive, physically or verbally. Usually in the moderate or severe stages. Why? Literature says that the dementia folks (correctly or incorrectly) believe their rights are being infringed upon. The loved ones' good intentions are misinterpreted, and thus mistrust slips in. Psychological inhibitions are diminished. Sleep issues factor in, as do reactions to medications and changes in routine. Some dementia folks have hallucinations as symptoms, along with depression and loneliness.

When my new granddaughter is uncomfortable, hungry, or wet—she knows to cry. Though she has no other memory or experience to tell her so, she has the instinct to rectify what needs to be. With dementia, I suppose, the memories which create these internal defenses dissolve, leaving reactions unguarded, unfiltered, causing in me the emotions of a more sensitive sort. 100 online prayers blew the circuits of the Uglies, and that is the Creator's victory. This victory, like lilies grown in cement, is a miracle.

"I am deeply grateful for my capacity to love me, which then extends outward.

Thankful to realize I am perfect, whole and complete, at my core."

Deborah Perdue

— Discussion, Thoughts, and Prayers —

1. Do you have a way to remind yourself to say 'I'm sorry, or 'Forgive me. I don't want to do that again'?

2. What crisis strategy do you guys have?

CHAPTER 14:

Then Came Easter

I've learned that family get-togethers are glue, regardless of all the things that happen or don't happen in the time between seeing each other. As someone with dementia, I've been weighing some of my new options.

The first family wedding happened in the first year after my diagnosis. Looking back, I realize now it was the hardest year of all. I decided not to go. It was too much, I explained, and most people understood what I meant. I was intimidated by the prospect of multiple conversations and the ensuing disorientation. I'd been no stranger to rejecting invitations, but this time it was my own embarrassment and fear of being different. I wasn't sure who I had become, nor was I sure that I could manage the New Dallas, especially in a busy public setting.

The next family get-together was Christmas. I bailed again. Then came Easter. I was getting used to being demented. I knew to stay away from the crowds and multiple conversations. I knew to stay away from the TV, as I can't process it for more than a few minutes. But, it was time to stop feeling as if there was no one of value left after the Old Dallas had gone. Sometimes, I could still get in a wisecrack or pejorative question, but that was the New Dallas pretending that the Old Dallas was still fully operational. It was dawning on me that pretending was a waste of time—it took too much concentration and energy. My jokes wound up ill-timed, delivered woodenly, in a tone too dark and a volume too strong. My acting job was poor. After one particular blunder, I had to call my buddy, Betty, the next day and ask her if I'd offended her. She wouldn't admit it, but I knew. I did know she didn't take it to heart.

At Easter, we stayed for three hours. There was great food, and it was so nice to see everyone, but I tried too hard to be the Old Dallas. Instead of appreciating the moment, I tried to participate actively, or create new moments. I was so exhausted that I almost felt the way I used to feel when I was drunk—disconnected, a bit irrational, inappropriate, losing track of time and space and perspective.

But today, I tried another family wedding. I went to the church ceremony. It was lovely. Beautiful music. One person talking at a time. Then we drove to the hotel and I stayed behind, opting out of going to the reception. But I put my own music on. I told Sonia to tell those who were wondering that I am the happiest I've ever been. It's true. But I do sometimes feel a little lonely or left out, or a yearning for the Old Dallas. The New Dallas misses him a bit, but I'm also more at peace, I am drawing closer to God more and more, I love my wife and kids more deeply, and I am getting to know myself better than ever before.

While I was listening to the music in my own personal reception, my daughter, Alia, and her husband, Doug, along with their daughter—my granddaughter—Adelaide, spent the day of that wedding across the country in their adopted hometown of Denver. They spent hours moving to a new house, in a foot of snow. It will take a little while to get used to, but it will be good because it is part of God's plan for them. Me, Dallas, old and new, will get used to it all, too. (Another digression as dementia symptoms grew. LOL)

"One can't believe impossible things," Alice said.
"I daresay you haven't had much practice,"
said the Queen.
"When I was your age, I always did it for half
an hour a day. Why, sometimes I've believed as
many as six impossible things before breakfast."

Lewis Carroll

CHAPTER 15:

Merry Dementia

To say—as some do—that the holidays and dementia don't mix, is not fully true. The idea misses the subtleties and the grey areas. Dementia people are not, of course, spiritless or joyless. There is a grand lie told, that no memory means no feelings, or that limited executive decision-making equals no ability to care or to enjoy. Dementia folks enjoy lesser things (lesser in the eyes of the cognitive world, of course)—a visit, a song, a touch, a joke, a good meal, a gift encased in glistening red wrapping wrapper. Conversely, there certainly exist holiday parties that can be awful for the dementia folks. The equivalent in the natural world to being tied to your chair in a concert hall to listen to the most loudly discordant orchestra, each instrument competitively playing their own song. The maestro acknowledges nothing. He keeps imaginary time with a stern smile on his face.

Holding the bags of presents for the cousins, I weaved through the parked cars toward the front door, wincing at the dozens of folks I could see through the adjacent windows, enjoying conversations. As the door opens, the sounds all merge into one indistinguishable cacophony, the only sound rising above the rabble is the persistent yip, yip, yip, yip, yip, yip, yip of a small lap dog dressed in antler ears. Yip, yip, yip, yip, yip, yip, she goes, turning in concordant circles in attempts to get under and in between my feet.

Merry Christmas! How are you doing? I think to myself, are they just using these words as a greeting, or are they referencing the dementia? I take off my coat and eye the environment—there is no quiet corner or chair where I can sit and smile and deflect the incoming deluge. Are you familiar with the board game Scrabble? You have to create words using letters you've chosen at random and then fit those words somehow onto the board, already filling with you and your opponent's previous attempts. Imagine playing six games simultaneously with six different opponents. Time buzzers are going off simultaneously, signaling that your decision-making is too slow. Going from person to person at a Christmas party is just as charged.

To add to the stereophonic mush, the yip, and the How Are You's, holiday music and a TV blare, both fighting the conversational noise and resulting in a three-way tie for dominance. As the glob starts accumulating in my head, my conversation grows increasingly banal. Words are replaced by a nod or a thumbs up. Crusty confusion mounts until I'm not sure I can figure out my next move physically because I am overwhelmed mentally. The only time I've felt like this before is during a thunderous full-court press in a packed gymnasium during a basketball game. You can barely speak because no one can hear over the din. You trust only your cognition, which is being tempted to abandon you, leaving only panic, telling you just throw the ball up in the air and go home. At the holiday party, I hit my max in 15 minutes. It's time to go home.

To all those caregivers out there, it's not much easier for you. No one asks about your life, it's always how is he doing and your reply must be a word or two for those who are easily satisfied. It's somewhere along the lines of other perilous questions: How's the divorce going? Did you get a job yet? How is your son doing in jail? How are your cancer treatments going? The burden is put on those answering, while the questioner languishes under the guise of thoughtfulness.

It's the season of multiple, simultaneous conversations—kryptonite for dementia folks. Though the holidays are advertised—rightly so—as difficult for dementia folks and caregivers, it's not all gloom and doom. It can be a time of remembered tenderness. Dementia memories vanish first from the present, last from the past. So in a quieter environment, families can feast on the bounty of old recollections. My daughters each gave me a gift of eternal proportions. Alia played me a tune we used to sing together as a duet in the car when she was young—Ariel sent me recordings of her first songs she wrote that carry a youth in her voice that soothes the soul in a fervent past. And watching the granddaughter giggle to the same blowtorch tummy tickles and lip strumming, cheek popping bag of tricks created a certain security in its perpetuity. Happiness is the fruit, shared memories the seeds.

Did I mention food? That Sonia can cook is an understatement. Apple pie, crown lamb, gluten-free pizza, omelets, pork sandwiches. It is miraculous food that satisfies before, during, and after the meal itself.

Just being with folks—even if the stage is smaller—can't be beat. The essence of family—knowing each other in all the brokenness over decades—makes our worlds serene for a time. Our footing is solid and sure, while the world spins in celebratory action. The world slings its arrows of trials and the devil orchestrates tragedy to remind us all that the world, in the end, cannot be relied upon for more than a moment at a time. But, dementia or not, those moments are divine.

— Discussion, Thoughts, and Prayers —

1. What is your family strategy for holidays and other family functions?

CHAPTER 16:

Never Been Happier

In the context of early stage dementia and Alzheimer's, the words 'I've never been happier' immediately create confusion. Unless of course, you have dementia.

Alzheimer's and happiness create different pictures in our brains. For many folks, dementia conjures nothing to the mind but a bedridden nursing home patient who can't recognize the few visitors she has from time to time. Alzheimer's and dementia actually begin with difficulties at home and work, then progresses over the years until cognition may go dim and empty. But, music, a good meal, invigorating exercise, handholding, and smiles remain joyful.

The secret of dementia is that it can give you a Get Out of Jail Free card. When it came to work, I was of the type to never unclench my fist. I secretly believed that retirement meant giving up on life, or on purpose. I no longer have the worries and deadlines from the law office, the school, the home budget, the need to win—all of which had become daily burdens. There is the gift of time. There is the gift of no more juggling while walking the edge of a cliff. How could those not be a benefit? How could this not create happy points?

Now there is time: to appreciate the outdoors, to appreciate my wife and my girls, time to make the bed, time to hear God speak in a whisper, time to enjoy a song played over and over, time to forget which day it is, time to read, time to think, time to reach out and reconcile, time to prepare to die—financially, legally, emotionally, time to answer questions that have been nagging at me for answers for years, time to walk, time to write, time to reflect, time to be thankful, time to be prayerful, time to be joyful, time to take a nap, time to snuggle, time to teach about dementia, time to wander, time to talk to the hummingbirds, time to exercise twice a day, time to cook, time to reach out to friends long since lost in time, time to sit, time to smile, time to be available to the Creator.

*"Trusting your heart means realizing
that your heart has access to a wisdom that is
many times greater than your intellect."*

Michael Bernard Beckwith

— Discussion, Thoughts, and Prayers —

1. What makes each of us happy?

2. How can we make it happen?

CHAPTER 17:

Job Hunting

I've never really liked the idea of hiring someone to help clean the house. I always thought that everyone should clean their own house, though in the old days—pre-dementia—I was actually quite the slob, and so cleaning was regrettably left to Sonia and the kids, along with Betty, my sister-in-law's Mom. She cleaned and we became friends because you didn't have to talk in code with her.

But now, with dementia, cleaning the house has become one of my top priorities. I can go at my pace. I don't have to talk or listen. I can still have pride in a job well done—and it's great exercise. My world is shrinking. It's smaller and slower, less global, there is less multi-tasking, and my endeavors have become more comfortable and satisfying. I'm not sure why, but I now like cleaning more than I remember liking arguing a trial in a courtroom. I like doing yard work, too. It's better than teaching a special education algebra class. I like folding my wife's pajamas and laying them folded on her pillow after they have come out of the dryer.

This, of course, has astounded my wife. For thirty-three years she picked up after me, sublimated her disappointment in my sense of personal hygiene, and rode the bucking bull of my arrogance. I considered my life, my vision, my office, my school, and my politics to be more valuable than the laundry. So, I must thank dementia once again. Go figure.

Ruth—the woman who now comes and cleans every two weeks—was referred by my wife's sister. When my wife, Sonia, hired Ruth, she mentioned that I had dementia, which didn't exactly translate to Russian, instead the word was lost somewhere along the way and became equated to lunatic, and for the first few scheduled appointments, she was a little reluctant to start work.

So, the ensuing story goes like this. On Ruth's first official visit, my wife is upstairs getting ready for work as Ruth and I engage in our first conversation.

"Can I ask you a question?" I inquired.

Ruth doesn't answer, but her face is wary.

"The rugs look so good after you vacuum them," I say. "When I do it, it doesn't look nearly so smooth."

Ruth breathes a sigh and starts off in accented English. She is showing me vacuum strokes while talking about old rugs and bad vacuums, both of which she is saying we have, though she doesn't want to be impolite. She is talking quickly, and my mind can't process the information fast enough to solve the mystery, but at least Ruth doesn't seem to think I'm a lunatic anymore. I hope.

*"New beginnings. New creations.
Our God is a God of all things new."*

Candance Crabtree

CHAPTER 18:

Mid-Stage Giggles

Dementia is funny, in a head-scratching sort of way. It's also funny in a ha-ha way. My wife doesn't think so. For her, any moment of humor morphs into a moment of worry and dread of the future. In many ways, dementia is way harder for the folks who are responsible for our care. I don't always quite know how to be supportive, helpful, or reassuring.

Do you know how I know I've arrived at the middle stages of dementia? Here are a few of my mid-stage experiences. I regularly send letters to two Fisher students currently in jail. I had been sending them $20 a month, along with a picture from Maine that they'd begun to put up on their wall of their cell. I loved getting their responses, too.

Writing them is a little tougher because I don't remember the threads of our ongoing pen-pal conversation, so I often need to go back and research our old letters. One of these former students, Lou, wrote: "Thanks for the money order, but you only sent the receipt. LOL." Ha! The other former student, Joe, wrote: "Thanks for the Maine picture, but you have sent the same one three times."

These days, my memory instantly discards the substance and sequence of a phone or face-to-face conversation. I will be in the middle of a story or offering some news, and then find myself suddenly marooned and weightless on dementia island, without the knowledge of how I arrived and unable to return. I should just admit the marooning, but that's a little like admitting you wet your pants in first grade. The shame trumps all.

Another signal of my mid-stage progression: I was on the phone with an old friend who had recently undergone a successful quadruple bypass surgery. I asked him if he called his brother. His response, "You dumbass, he died three weeks ago." Whoops.

Some folks assume that my dementia has affected my hearing, since I'm constantly asking What did you say? Sometimes people think they're being helpful when they shout for clarity, but it actually scares the bejesus out of me. It's not a hearing problem, but rather a processing one; I often miss the beginning of sentences, and then the words mount up so quickly.

Now for my last tale. I was cutting lawns the other Sunday and I got poison ivy on my hands, so I wore gloves so as not to spread or scratch it. A friend told me he suspected I had gotten worse and that I thought it was winter already. Ha! Come on. That's funny. Other small details that mark my place in the solidly mid-stages of dementia? I've recently succumbed to the pill case that delineates days, along with a.m. and p.m. designations. When I send my handwritten work to my typist and friend, Cheryl, I usually don't remember what I wrote after about an hour or two of sending it. When she sends it back, I don't remember writing it. It is like a surprise gift.

"Those who hope in the Lord will renew their strength. They will soar on wings like eagles; they will run and not grow weary, they will walk and not be faint. "

Isaiah 40:31

CHAPTER 19:

Howard Howard

I just love when the real world and the dementia world meld together. I'm not sure why I get a kick out of it. I'm getting used to the subtleties and speed of the dementia world. One of the most fun things to do is throw down penalty flags as normal people, who do not know how to speak dementia, muddle a conversation. For example, a foul: when a normal person interrupts a demented person to make a point, then waits for a follow-up or reply to their point, while incorporating remarks of mine, which I now can't remember. Here's where the penalty flag is thrown: you can't speak that way with a dementia person. Our short-term memory and organizational skills are compromised. Multi-layered, stop and go conversation might as well be another language.

With that in mind, here is my story. I recently went to the public library where I sometimes volunteer for brief, two-hour stints. It's a small town, a small library, and I probably can't mess things up too much. Nevertheless, I am always a little apprehensive. I just don't know the library's environment well, or how it will mesh or not mesh with my dementia. All the same, I am thinking my odds are good. For the first few minutes, I try to step back into this real world; I try to be a big shot, do it on my own. Here's a good time to interject Proverbs 3:5-6: "Trust in the Lord with all your heart, and lean not on your own understanding. In all ways acknowledge him, and he will make your paths straight." So, let me tell you how it worked out relying on my own wits rather than on Godly wisdom. With my peacock tail starting to fan out, I go up the stairs a little stiffly and old looking.

"You must be Dallas?" I hear. I assume the man speaking is the man I'm meant to meet, my boss for the day. No one else is at the library, so it doesn't take a rocket scientist to make this assumption.

"My name is Howard Howard," he says.

This was perplexing.

I'm trying to figure out if he's pulling my leg, or if

he said the name Howard twice, as if I didn't hear it the first time. At this, my face must look a bit puzzled, maybe even a little bit distraught. He nicely went on to explain that his name is Howard Howard because he was adopted. I've thought about this for a few days. I'm pretty sure being adopted is irrelevant to the story of how he got the name Howard Howard. If it somehow is relevant, the story still has got to shed the light on why someone would give this dude the lifelong burden of explaining his name every time he met someone.

After that brief explanation, I was left wondering whether I was somehow mistaken, that perhaps my dementia had progressed and I wasn't able to figure out just what was going on with the whole Howard Howard thing. I had no choice but to move on, completely unable to discern what just happened. Howard Howard taught me a lot about the library. On the way out for the day, I thanked him, but to my surprise—and to his—I confessed I had forgotten his name! Of all names to forget, Howard Howard seemed an unlikely option. (I think I made the exit up in my head. LOL)

Later, I reflected on Howard Howard's burden, and why he seemed so pleased to shock me with the unconventionality of his name while maintaining such a straight face. Why couldn't he just say his name was Howard and save the Howard Howard duo for a second date?

I think if I ever went back to work there, I would change my name to Howard, too, so I could introduce myself as Howard, and then introduce you to my boss, Howard Howard. In that event, I hope no dementia people come into the library.

"Trust in the Lord with all your heart, and lean not on your own understanding.
In all ways acknowledge him, and he will make your paths straight."

Proverbs 3:5-6

— Discussion, Thoughts, and Prayers —

1. What are your weekly and daily schedules?

2. Is it time to freshen them up? Even a little?

CHAPTER 20:

A View

The View. No, not the television show. A view. You know, what vacations are for, or the observation deck of the Empire State Building, or starry nights, red sunsets, waves showing their white hair in the wind. A view is bigger than all of us.

When I was first diagnosed with dementia, I asked my neurologist what was left when we become vegetables. I rolled my eyes, unimpressed, when he coughed out, "That's a philosophical question." I used to be derisive of him, but now, as my own dementia quickens its progression, I'm just sad for him and others that forget the power of a view.

We all have known a view that touches more than our mind, more than our memory. The pictures of our wedding, our family get-togethers, our kid's first day of school, graduation day—these are all powerful sights to our mind and memory, special gifts that we value above all else. If there is ever a fire, I'm grabbing the photo albums or, in this day and age, the cell phone stocked with pictures. Either way, money could never compensate for the memories that grow even sweeter as time goes by and we near closer to the end of our lives.

A view, on the other hand? The pictures and memories of it leave us less than fully refreshed. Being there in person to see it again continues to gently evoke something quite different than our cognition. Is it our heart? Is it our soul? Our spirit? Our hearts and spirits are so different from one another's, aren't they? They have been broken, tested, warmed by love in different ways and to different degrees and at different moments of our lives. They are ever changing, linked to our choices and experiences, weaknesses and illnesses.

No matter who you are, no matter when, a view touches all of us. We may choose to turn away or discount it or pretend it bypasses us or is of no interest or relevancy, but it has been seen. It has touched something deeper than our minds, if only for a curious instant. It landed in our souls without our permission, like God breathing life into Adam and all of mankind. It is a reminder of something bigger. Something that is not brain, memory, or personality driven. It simply is. We can't invent it, reproduce it, bottle it, or put it on TV.

— Discussion, Thoughts, and Prayers —

1. Got a favorite view?

2. Do you have favorite places or people to visit for fun: Baseball stadiums, gardens, or your grandkids?

CHAPTER 21:

Demented:
One Year from Diagnosis

A different Dallas. I was diagnosed with dementia in May 2014, and as of this writing, it's been about a year since my initial diagnosis. It's taken some time to figure out my body—more specifically my brain—and how it influences my everyday existence. One year later I say, matter of fact, that I can't keep up with the person I'm most used to being with— my wife. What does not being able to keep up mean? If I was on crutches, the phrase would ring a bit more literally, but mentally it works like this: If she interrupts me, I forget what my line of thinking was. if she switches subjects too abruptly, or threads together two lines of conversation simultaneously, I cannot track it.

My bandwidth has narrowed. When we researched it, the Internet provided an illustration using just that word, bandwidth. It was used almost fleetingly within a larger thought – something like he did not have the bandwidth to have a relationship with her at that point in time. It hit a little too close to home. Conversations other than short ones, or ones where I was not fresh from a nap, felt like running in sand for me. I found myself getting off the phone with a poorly disguised sense of urgency, bordering on rude. Sometimes it felt like swimming—that I might go under if I didn't grapple for the sides of the pool.

I begin to track the occurrences when I cannot summon a particular word or phrase, and realize that these moments have become somewhat routine. Sometimes, accompanied by a strange hilarity, a word not at all related to my intended phrase pops out. The disappearing memory tank, where something that occurred quite recently ventures down the rabbit hole never to return. When it happens now it is easy to discern, easy to ignore, easy not to get all too excited over. I no longer broadcast it as a show-stopping moment, a specific marker in devolution. I merely tuck it away with a wink to myself.

Lack of conversation during the day is refreshing. Exercise is still the best elixir. Alcohol, on the other hand, gives me hot flashes, and hay fever medicines are a no-no. I lost half a day trying one of those. Namenda doesn't bother me, but I stopped taking Aricept because it caused muscle cramps, which might affect my NBA draft chances.

There were days with mini-bouts of electricity shortages, and some of those are gone. The Dracula fog of tiredness still descends after lunch and then again at around eight. I work on my writing three hours every morning, but that last half hour feels like a race against time.

When I first went to a dementia support group in February 2015, one guy told me that all he does every day is watch the Weather Channel. I looked at him as we were leaving the hospital's meeting area, thinking he was kidding. He had been diagnosed two or three years prior. At the time it seemed somehow an incongruous comment, but I see now from where it comes.

I have been tempted to sacrifice everything–relationships, activities – for peace for my brain. It's dangerous. Even small deviation from routine can be enjoyable.

Confusion is uncomfortable. Forgetfulness is frustratingly inconvenient. Together they make a dangerous cocktail, because you can forget how to upend your confusion, or you forget how to enjoy the moments of clarity without remembering the decline.

I've written before about the experience of sharing your diagnosis with others, and how common the response is for the other person to start doing their own self-inventory, wondering if the keys they misplaced last week was, in fact, an indicator of a larger problem. But think of it this way: consider a magic trick—you place an item inside the hat and it disappears. When you have dementia, it is as if the item hidden beneath the scarf was never there to begin with—the memory of the objects is gone. So when the hat is tipped and out returns the missing object—the misplaced keys, perhaps—someone with dementia would be genuinely surprised. How did they get there at all?

"Oh, Great Spirit, I awake to another sun, grateful for gifts bestowed, granted one by one."

Twylah Nitsch

— Discussion, Thoughts, and Prayers —

1. Do either of you keep a journal?

2. Do you schedule times just to be, to talk about small things?

CHAPTER 22:

Demented Folks are a Big Pain in the Butt

I can't deny that I have been hard-headed, judgmental, self-absorbed—someone who always thinks he is right. As an athlete, politician, lawyer, and school principal, the number of people I have silently or verbally insulted or demeaned is too many to remember. I am truly sorry for my arrogance. But, my flaws alone do not fully explain why I, or demented folks in general, have a reputation for being a big pain in the butt.

In the later stages of our disease, we are sometimes known to be violently oppositional. To those who are committed to caring for us, that's a dangerous and scary proposition. So it seems only fair that I explain my own behavior, in particular, the stubbornness that stems from dementia. I hope my explanation can help.

Firstly, I've observed in myself the tendency to fixate on issues that were once pretty unimportant in the grand scheme of things. For example, these days I am frequently concerned with whether or not we have enough laundry detergent left. This is a relatively harmless fixation unless someone else has forgotten to pick it up on the way home from work, and then it is as if someone I deeply trust has left our children at the pizza parlor overnight—I'm horrified. Even though I can no longer work or drive, I have not relinquished my need to contribute to the family, so instead my energy—and all that goes along with it— has attached itself to the laundry duties. The laundry has become my measure of success, and when you mess with my latest passion, you have essentially stomped on world peace. By that logic, my reaction and indignity, my sense of betrayal, are quite real; it's just not real by real world standards. In the world of dementia, emotion runs deceptively deep and rises to the surface without much warning.

All the associated literature on dementia says that emotion and memory have an intrinsic relationship, so that when we get upset our memory becomes even more bruised. When we get upset, the holes of memory multiply, which exacerbates our annoyance at the initial loss. If you and I are having a conversation and you innocently interrupt me mid-thought to share a timely comment, the conversation is likely to explode (from our dementia point of view). It is because we have forgotten the thread of the conversation before the interruption.

There are other emotional components to dementia; it's not solely about memory. We are shedding the world that we built over the years. In just five months I stopped practicing law, stopped managing my finances, stopped going to seminary, stopped driving, stopped visiting former students in jail, closed the Emily Fisher Family Center, stopped going to my old church, stopped looking for work. All of these moves have lightened the load on my brain, but have also lightened my spirit. I am joyful when I ride my bike. I am joyful as I tighten the screws on the stairway railing. I am joyful as I bring my wife her coffee in the morning.

Dementia can make us sometimes bad-tempered, but it can also make us peaceful, joyful, and thankful if we remember who we are and don't mix it up with who we were. And what are we becoming? I'll let you know.

– *Discussion, Thoughts, and Prayers* –

1. When are the times not so good?

2. What strategies do you have to avoid the bad times or to get through them quickly?

CHAPTER 23:

Do You Speak Dementia?

My granddaughter, Adelaide Dallas Rolwood—just over a year old—speaks excellent dementia. Conversing with Adelaide is much more fun than talking about the weather forecast with me, George Dallas Dixon. Her language is unencumbered by cognition, self-editing, or worse – deception, feigned interest, divided attention, obfuscation, or pointless space-filling small talk meant to avoid the discomfort of silence. Her language is not the language of our world. Hers is the wail of discomfort, the sparkle of engagement, the glee of surprise, and the peace of a simple connection. Of course, there is cognitive input, but the exchange delights both sides of the connection, emanating from a deeper, purer place that we have mostly forgotten until we are joyfully reminded of it by a child.

This same joy is possible for both the person with dementia and his or her family. To tap into this simplest of joys, we must shut off our practiced, worldly cognitive habits and recognize that the same unencumbered back-and-forth can evoke tenderness and smiles. Of course, It's natural to desire the established modes of conversation and connection between ourselves and the spouse with dementia, the parent with dementia, and the like. But we must go back to a mode of communication that we are no longer used to, a simpler sort, but a kind that is still able to create a spark. This sort of communication need not advance step-by-step to a cognitive conclusion, as we have become accustomed to. Instead, the conversational end game is as simple as sharing.

'Tell me all about it' is such a good entry point to offer the demented person, but it is a gift that you can spoil if you focus on your own lack of understanding. Instead, crawl in next to it and snuggle with words from the heart, whether they have meaning for you or not. They have meaning—heartfelt, spiritual, and soulful meaning—for the person with dementia.

I worry out loud to my wife about where she will put me when I can no longer live at home. Many people believe that where a demented person ends up once they're in the final stages doesn't really matter, since the demented person likely won't cognitively know where he or she is. True enough.

But we will know where we are emotionally, in our hearts, and spiritually, in our souls. I believe that. Staring at a wall is a far cry from the view of sunset over the ocean between wispy layers of fog. Just like the power of conversation can sustain without cognition, so can the soulful warmth of a view be sustained without knowing which latitude and longitude you are at.

My current and favorite view is from a wooden porch in Gouldsboro, Maine. An island lies a mile away on the left. The trees are a variety of greens that turn red in the fall. The ocean between is always moving, giving away the direction and strength of the wind. The sea's hues vary in blueness, depending on its reflection in the clouds and the fog hovering above it. Birds of all kinds—yellow, blue, brown, and white, along with the great eagle and speedy hummingbirds—never cease to entertain. I say hello to Red, the hummingbird, almost every day. Chipmunks and squirrels, a deer, or a fat old porcupine visit on occasion, too. There is the constant smell of salt water. This view is connected to my spirit and soul, mostly bypassing mind or memory. This is my resting place; this is my small child gurgling with joy and peace. Join me on the porch and I'll show you how to speak dementia, like Adelaide, along with a lobster meal, and music for dessert.

"Peace I leave with you; my peace I give you. I do not give to you as the world gives. Do not let your hearts be troubled and do not be afraid."

John 14:27

— Discussion, Thoughts, and Prayers —

1. When are the times each of you could be more patient?

2. How do each of you show your love?

CHAPTER 24:

Undercover Dementia Man

The Portland Rehabilitation Center—as I'll call it in this chapter—is not a rehabilitation center. The physical therapy room has a set of parallel bars—and that's pretty much it. There is nothing else in the room. Not to mention, it took me two years to gain official entrance to the facility as a volunteer. Before I'd earned entry, I helped out in church—I helped folks find the right hymnal page and I called out the numbers at Bingo.

Yes, I am Dallas the volunteer. But in reality, I am Undercover Dementia Man. The facility knows that I have dementia, and I certainly put it on the paperwork, too. What're you doing here, Dallas the volunteer? Mabel is a resident who hands out the evening snacks to keep everyone's blood sugar stable, and was the one to ask me that. I couldn't quite tell her that I was here—in my own mind—to see what nursing home life was really like.

Big Kevin, the youngest person living there and the most vocal by far, is my inside partner and collaborator. He has insurgency written all over him. He interacts with the staff with an edge, one that's tinged with the unspoken threat that he too knows their secrets. He has been here for four years.

No, this is not a rehabilitation center; it's a nursing home of sixty-some odd beds, two to a room. When I walk in, no one asks me who I am or what I'm doing. Does that say something about the nursing home or does it say more about my undercover skills? I do have a sticker that reads Dallas—Volunteer. So, I just walk where I want to, looking as if I belong. It reminded me of when I used to walk into the gyms and food joints at Villanova College, pretending I was a freshman at the University, when I was actually a sophomore in high school. Maybe they knew all along. I don't think my cover is blown at the nursing home, even though the social worker, who now occupies the front office, said to me once,

"We are on the same wavelength, right?"

I replied, "Yep," but I had no idea what she was talking about.

I wanted to volunteer to see what dementia looks like in the next stage, and the life that folks have in a nursing home. Looking down that road is part of preparation. It's not depressing, although it probably occurred to you that this is all a bit macabre. But, the people are so full of character. The staff seems distant and veiled, a little zombie-like, but the folks that live here? Shirley was so apologetic that she had come to church in her pajamas. Maybe she has an eye on Captain Barry because she was really directing her apology to him, fully and decidedly. I've also bonded with Sue Ann. She is from Wisconsin and plays the violin. Her eyes are alive with wit and determination. "Sue Ann," the aide or another resident reminds her, "don't forget your walker." I don't know why they say this so often. It's probably simple – she may fall. But, she doesn't just ignore the advice, nor does she consider it. Her wit and response are lightning quick as she explains (technically), 'Why should I? I am not walking.' And she stands, deciding her next move.

— Discussion, Thoughts, and Prayers —

1. How can we help other families that are in the same situation?

2. Have you reached out to the local Alzheimers Association, the local dementia-friendly group, or checked out the <u>great</u> Teepa Snow videos?

CHAPTER 25:

Looking Back

The truth is this: after thirty-three years of marriage, I almost threw it all away in the first year after my formal diagnosis.

My attitude at the time could be summed up this way: I'm going to die sometime soon, so you need to get on with your life. I basically was instructing my wife to explore the world as a single, unattached person. I told her, I'm leaving New Jersey, and going to Maine to live a simpler life. You're welcome to visit, but I'm not sure I'm ever coming back. That's that.

But God came to me in a whisper, telling me that just because I have dementia didn't mean I was absolved of the responsibility and vow I committed to when my wife and I got married. I needed to get over myself, stop playing the victim, and recognize that there are a million tragedies out there that dwarf my predicament. God required that I surrender myself to him and his plan, rather than rely on my own shaky standing and mixed-up view of how I, and the world, ought to plan and behave.

So much has changed since I was first diagnosed with dementia. Measuring my expectations of the first year post-diagnosis versus the reality of how it all unfolded is a mind-boggling endeavor. During those first few months after my diagnosis, I did retreat to my coastal Maine cabin. Throughout that first year, I was sure that the emotional components of dementia were years away, somewhere far down the road in some other stage of this disease. Emotional outbursts, tears, unending stubbornness, chest-tightening anger. Looking back, so much of my interactions were colored by the terrible cocktail of suspect logic and overly sensitive emotions. It was a toxic version of myself, and when I sense it rearing its ugly head, I know a little bit of what to expect, and so I try to mitigate the potential fallout: I exercise, I pray, I try to keep me and my sharp edges out of the way. If I attempt to challenge this toxicity in any other way—particularly by trying to outsmart it with a brain that is faulty—it is like throwing grease on the fire.

A minor disappointment, an expectation reasonably unfulfilled, a mistake made by the world—any can act as a catalyst for this toxic state of mind. Being tired doesn't help; it lets the Uglies creep in. I know that I can't beat it on my own, but somehow, every time, I can convince myself that my rationale is vindicated, that last time it was the Uglies and Toxic Dallas and the Dementia, but this time, I'm really right. What a mistake. I should know by now that I can't do it on my own. How many times must I relearn this lesson? Countless, the answer seems to be. (Written in August 2016).

"If you knew who walks beside you, fear would be impossible."

A Course in Miracles

CHAPTER 26:

B-12

I can quite easily recall my myriad uncool moments. While I was a college student, I went on my first date with a woman. We were walking back from a football game and while I was animatedly talking to her, I ran head first into a telephone pole. She kept walking a few steps before she even noticed. On another date, I drank too much and peed my pants. Not cool! I was subbing for someone in a soccer match, and as I pulled down my sweats to join the game in uniform, I made the mistake of also pulling my shorts down, showing my butt to the not small crowd. Another time, I went to sit down in my lawyer's chair in court, after quite an effective bail lowering argument. I missed the chair and the papers went flying like a Three Stooges movie. When my eldest daughter was born, the doctor asked whether I wanted to cut the umbilical cord as a sign of...whatever. I messed it up. I cut somewhere I shouldn't have, blood squirting everywhere. You probably get the point.

The latest moment:

The doctor recently told me to stop taking antacid stomach medicine, because it prevented the body's acids from absorbing B-12, a problem also attributed to a serious gluten allergy I have called Celiac disease. When the body cannot absorb B-12, it can mimic Alzheimer's and dementia-like symptoms.

So, I stopped taking the stomach medicine that blocked the B-12. I stayed cool, relatively cool, for a while. I was starting to remember little things, but didn't tell many people. Then, I was given a prescription for B-12 that I could give myself via injection. I've done it twice so far. How's this for a measurement. Last year, I averaged about four hours of writing per day. This year, I average about an hour and a half of writing per day. Since my doctor's B-12 advice, I started writing at 8:30 this morning and it is now 12:30, and I don't feel the least bit tired. Yesterday I watched the bike rental office for a friend, a full eight-hour day and without a nap, then

I went to bible study, my first time in a while. So, I've told my wife, in an understated sort of way, you know, trying to be cool. My head is screeching God, is this your gift? Playing it cool is not my strong suit. I don't deserve it.

Am I really cured? Can this be? Who can I call to share this news? Aahh. Wow. Thank you, God. Amazing. (No, not so cool, right?)

— Discussion, Thoughts, and Prayers —

1. Have you had your B-12 checked?

EPILOGUE

It's been six weeks and six shots of B-12. My black and white, two-dimensional world has transformed suddenly into a striking, multidimensional one. I hadn't noticed the downward trend in my vision in the past two years that I'd been slogging through dementia. It's not until now, as things sharpen into focus, that I recognize how complete the difference is. What has happened since has not suddenly made me believe in God's personal touch in my life. That's been true since I made the decision that God is real, experientially—not just conceptually. It's not unlike the sureness that wells within you when you know you are in love, or when you sense someone looking at you, and you turn your gaze up, and sure enough, you were right. But what happened supersized my awe and my commitment to love God each day.

It all started with organic licorice. No, it began with Sonia making me see Dr. Newman when I went to live in Maine. No, it started when Sonia got me into spin classes to stabilize my dementia decline. Doc had me stop my daily Prevacid dose because it prevents the body from properly absorbing B-12. Until then, I had been double dosing Prevacid for thirty years. When I finally stopped and started leaning on the organic licorice—a natural soother of gastrointestinal issues—I started remembering things, moments of clarity unexpectedly rising to the surface like tiny bubbles.

At the lowest point of my dementia, around summer 2016, a moment came when I couldn't remember what year it was. I decided, with assurance, that it was 2013.

After stopping the Prevacid, I called my doctor. I said, "Doc, something is going on. I'm remembering things that I couldn't before." I went to his office and was prescribed weekly injections of B-12, 100cc in each shot. I can now watch movies, stay up until 10 p.m., write all day, remember verbal instructions for what to buy at the supermarket, and drive my car. My memory feels refreshed, but the emotional consequences of dementia—insecurity, distrust, being too easily disappointed, overreacting to grey-area situations—stubbornly remain, unfortunately. But yesterday I played basketball, the first time in a long time. The last time I played, I'd struggled to remember which team I was on. Sometimes my perception of time is still skewed, but nowhere near so far off base that I mistake the year for 2013 again.

The symptoms of a B-12 deficiency look a lot like the symptoms of vascular dementia and Alzheimer's. But when it comes to B-12 deficiency, cognitive function that is compromised—memory problems, executive functioning—can be restored (sometimes partially) with proper treatment, assuming the condition was not left untreated for too long. My doctor instructed me to wait three months to determine how sweeping this new cognitive restoration may be, but it's possible that I might not know anything definitively for at least a few years. It's even possible that my condition is some combination of B-12 deficiency, vascular dementia, or Alzheimer's, rather than just one or the other.

So, two years plus of dementia. Potentially misdiagnosed. Do I sue? No doctor I saw considered B-12 as the perpetrator, though my deficiency spanned years. But, all the same, the lynchpin is this: there were things I liked and valued about dementia. I had time to evaluate where I have been and where I was headed. I had more time to spend with God. I made new friends. I took up exercise with a renewed fervor. Of course, on the home front, my wife was shouldering much of the ugly particulars—I drifted further and further away from her, emotionally, physically, and she took up the difficult and consuming task of managing me, the household duties, and a full-time job. She managed to sell our house, draft power of attorney documents, handled the finances, and learn to be alone without being consumed by loneliness.

I can't believe God is random. For two years, I waded through the throes of dementia for a reason. If that reason is because I'm meant to dedicate my remaining years to those with dementia, I'm in. No matter how turbulent the storm, I'm in. I'm so full of joy when God is working in my life—not because it's deserved, or because of anything that I've done. I've never prayed for a cure. It's funny, when I tell this story, most folks just believe the dementia has really gotten worse and that I'm probably nuts. Understandable. But, enjoy God with me. I leave the future in God's hands. I surrender. I would mess things up trying to do it on my own.

God has made a mess into a miracle. I believe that

God works with purpose, and I believe that two years of experiencing dementia has positioned me to be of unique help to others. I spent time with the residents of the North Portland Nursing Home and learned the opportunity inherent in dementia. To me, dementia was not a horror show, but a chance to become unwed from traditional cognition. At the nursing home, Laverne said that the hymn we sang was her all-time favorite, and she glowed with joy. Heart, soul, and strength are not lost to those with dementia. She went on to repeat the same sentiment four more times, which to some would read as a tragedy of the mind, but in fact resulted in four more episodes of total joy.

Where to now? God grew me through these two years, and if He is creating any sort of work for me, I accept it with gratitude.

" I will give thanks to you, Lord, with all my heart; I will tell of all your wonderful deeds."

Psalm 9:1

53602123R00084

Made in the USA
Middletown, DE
28 November 2017